Rebel Women

ALSO BY VANCY KASPER

POETRY
Mother, I'm So Glad You Taught Me How to Dance

Y.A. FICTION
Always Ask for a Transfer
Escape to Freedom
Street of Three Directions

Rebel Women

poems

Vancy Kasper

Inanna Poetry & Fiction Series

Inanna Publications and Education Inc.
Toronto, Canada

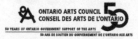

The publisher gratefully acknowledges the support of the Canada Council for the Arts and the Ontario Arts Council for its publishing program.

The publisher is also grateful for the kind support received from an Anonymous Fund at The Calgary Foundation.

Front cover artwork: Andrea Kollo, "Remembrance: God Bless the Fallen," photograph, 2009. <www.andrea-kollo.com>.

Library and Archives Canada Cataloguing in Publication
Kasper, Vancy, author
        Rebel women / Vancy Kasper.

Poems.
Issued in print and electronic formats.
ISBN 978-1-926708-96-6 (bound) — ISBN 978-1-926708-97-3 (pdf)

        1. Canada — History — Rebellion, 1837-1838 — Poetry. I. Title.
PS8571.A86R43 2013   C811'.54   C2013-902591-X
                                          C2013-902592-8

Printed and bound in Canada

Inanna Publications and Education Inc.
210 Founders College, York University
4700 Keele Street
Toronto, Ontario, Canada M3J 1P3
Telephone: (416) 736-5356 Fax (416) 736-5765
Website: www.inanna.ca   Email: inanna.publications@inanna.ca

for Paul Litt, historian and Shepard family cousin
for his material and support, and for Fred

for Silvia and Fred Jr., for Esther and Max

Contents

In search of my mother's garden I found my own.
                    —Alice Walker, poet and novelist

Introduction

These poems began with my grandmother's stories, passed down from her mother, her aunts and her friends. Today women are largely left out from most documentation about the 1837 Rebellion. But as a child, my grandmother's stories helped me to understand the determination of women never to buckle under — be it intimidation, Rebellion, threats, gossip or death.

Then other voices came — mother, father, aunts. Poems flowed on, through my family, circling friends and dear ones no longer here.

Historical Notes

In 1837, Toronto was divided politically into Loyalist Torys (Conservatives) led by the powerful Family Compact, and Loyalist Reformers, led by William Lyon Mackenzie. Both were legitimate political parties.

The Family Compact refused to compromise on any issue and was petty and vindictive to its critics. Reformers were encouraged to do likewise. Sir Francis Bond Head was the unpopular Lieutenant Governor.

Reformers, comprised of butchers, millers and blacksmiths, found they could not collect any debts from the Family Compact, their biggest customer, even if they had won a judgment in court.

By 1837 there was no longer a safety valve for discontent through the elected body, the Legislative Assembly. Prior to that, citizens displeased with actions of the Family Compact, could vent frustrations through the Assembly. It could issue condemnations of Family Compact measures and block the oligarchy's legislative proposals. There was also the right of appeal to the Colonial Office and the British Government. But in the election of 1836 the Reformers were soundly defeated. They ascribed this to interference by the new governor, Francis Bond Head, and his advisors.

The summer election that year was the last straw. Mackenzie was running again as the Reform candidate. Bond Head and the Family Compact distributed tickets giving title to farms on Lakeshore Road and in the bush, where no one knew there were farms. Holders went to the polls and swore they got four dollars out of farms they did not own. But they swore enough crooked votes to beat the Reformers, who all owned property in the country. Mackenzie was defeated annd leading Reformers knew then that they would have to fight.

Most Reformers had gone beyond the stage of clearing the land and building a home. Their leaders, Mackenzie, Duncombe, Lount, Shepard and others, were widely respected and encouraged fellow Reformers to take up arms. In most cases, they did this by playing down the highly illegal nature of what they were proposing. Instead, they emphasized the moral rightness of their actions and the dangers of not taking action. Since armed demonstrators had marched successfully in England in support of the Great Reform Bill a few years earlier and won, they felt an armed but peaceful demonstration would result in a more democratic government and wouldn't be very different.

But armed Rebellion is an act of treason.

It's better to die on your feet than to live on your knees.
—Dolores Ibarruri, Spanish Communist leader

Statira Montgomery Willson, sister of John Montgomery
(Montgomery's Tavern), great-great-grandmother of Vancy Kasper.

Rebel Women

for Catherine

There are herbs, Catherine,
my Great-Great Grandmother was told —
tansy can slow a heart,
hibernate the trouble.

She had tied a Rebel ribbon around
her son's arms and knew it was too early
to roll the Christmas pies
— apple, sparse crabapple.
Give us this day, our daily —
slap hard on the board for
Mrs. Lount, 30 miles north-east —
her arms aching from the waving,
roll and roll for Mrs. Matthews.
The Lord is our Shepherd
Does she have a letter too?
Crouching between candlesticks,
sealed against defeat, penned
by her sons, like mine?
Anointest their heads with oil,
flute the apples for Mrs. Anderson.

Dear God, do we have enough pennies for the eyes?

The icy ground between the oak and birch
is thickened by their Rebel sons,
their fathers, brothers and husbands,
who stumble with courage — towards York.

Forgive them their trespasses

Eerie winds this December
deafen these Rebel mothers, wives and sisters
with pitchforks under, pies on, their tables.
They do not look out
at wind and ice bending pines
wood for coffins.

Catherine Shepard, January 1838

My Great-Great Grandmother's sleep
bubbles with the lies of yesterday's headlines
vilifying her Shepard lineage.
She will not run.
She will not leave.
She firms her loose bowels with cheese
and swallows salt to still her fluttering throat.
She does not crochet.

Her black wool bonnet and skirt,
so empty of Joseph's heat,
still carry the whiff of his coffin ground.
They are not tied and fastened with poems
but by hands calloused
from casting musket balls.
She, above all, cannot sidle east,
sneak south into Toronto.

A Shepard does not flee.
She gathers her firm flesh to her stuttering womb,
bridles, and backs horses to the wagon.
Today she will ride slowly
— 15 miles straight down Yonge Street —
down this Family Compact Street,
past men who spit on the ground at her,

past women whose sons might have been killed by her sons,
one month ago in the Rebellion.
She forges iron into her backbone,
juts her chin.

It's the distance from like Rebel women
she mourns the most.
Their fear-lined faces have etched cravasses
through her dreams. They rise in
her nights, drift to alien towns, they are
last to be served. Their yeast and flour
short-weighted and pawed. Mocked,
they have buried their men, their children.
Their conquerors know they cannot leave.

Catherine, mother of five Shepard Rebels,
wraps bread, bundles salt pork.
Conspicuous and proud, she clicks the horses,
trots through defeat to the Toronto jail.
Joseph, her baby but one, and
steady Thomas, Jacob and Michael, wait
in the corner cell, and overlook the gallows.

She steps down, winds herself in her faith
 — enters the jail to beg —
and beg —
Beg.

What A Rebel Woman Knows

Wheat doesn't ruffle
in winter wind.
It lies shivering and waits
for her man's hand
to pry it out,coax it
to rise from its Newmarket knees at solstice —
and to grow high, to spite these Tories
gutted with drink,
who chase her pikeman
on the run so many nights;
him who stood firm at Montgomery's
without even a musket,
— not like some who went home.
She wades through ashes buttering her house,
thick as black ice on porch and window.
Her fat has gone to fear —
she lays her children down at night
on cold parlour floors,
vermilion night skies east and west
rank with smudge;
forcing her throat
into her lungs and she is dizzy.
Tory torches are coming her way.
She prays that acrid smell they bring
is not flesh.

Elizabeth Willson Shepard (1826-1885) (great-grandmother of Vancy Kasper)
and Stillwell Shepard (1856-1926) c.1858.

Bonny Catherine Shepard

Aye, Mrs. Joseph Shepard is bonny
with most of her own teeth
and that purple silk bonnet
from her cousin in Virginia. If you ask me,
husbands turn and stare too long
following her rare blue eyes.
Mrs. Shepard's hearth is brick —
not field stones stuck with oxshit.
Hers goes two floors up
straight to God
with a more reticent one
in the back kitchen.
Her house is board and batten,
flannelled walls,
not logs.

You might see me borrow
some dried apples from Mrs. Shepard
to get a glimpse
of that gold chamber pot
I've heard she pisses in.

Elizabeth Willson Shepard, great-grandmother of Vancy Kasper.

My Grandmother Crochets

My Grandmother Statira crochets.
She lives in one room,
its ceiling held up by poems:
Shakespeare, Shelley, Byron, Keats
and some American poets, whose books
she scrimped, sent away for,
given to me.

Every afternoon, sunlight
roils across her powdered face,
pasty and mottled with sweat.
She is not dead — she is hot.

Questions I don't ask:
Why is she in this room?
Is she the family's husk?
Has the T. Eaton wallpaper hidden her wings
and does having the biggest closet make her happy?

Her aches strangle each movement,
except her hands,
knuckles sharp with bony spurs,
that loop and whorl the thread.

Sometimes threads take detours,
stitches are misplaced, she says.

Except her eyes, blue with poems;
except her mind, rich with sashes and hasps,
pianos and violins.

She always follows the pattern.
Her heartbeat keeps up.
Her compass is correct.

An exile in our southwest bedroom,
she thinks of her Great Grandfather,
a fur trader, honoured by Algonquins, Ojibway.
The first and only white man in Lansing
who escaped bogs and mosquitoes
to erect York's first shanties at its
founding in 1793 —
claiming and homesteading
the North-west corner of Yonge and Sheppard.
She remembers the log house,
her birth house.

She is Kit, the Christmas baby,
second youngest of Joseph Shepard.
Listen child, she says when I dash
home from school, brush her cheek,
fidget foot to foot:
My mother hid, listened to their wild plans,

dangerous whispers.
She was just a teenager — she fled when
a musket ball dropped —

I'm backing away...

She heard a voice say Raise your pitchforks.
Tilt them for maiming.

I'm in the hall, down the stairs —

Aim dead centre, twist, withdraw.
Keep your forks. You need them for spring seeding.

I'm opening the front door —

Grandma's voice is faint —

Mother ran from Father's house —
Your Great Grandfather,
Justice of the Peace.

Out on the boulevard,
five blocks south of Montgomery's Tavern,
owned by my Great Uncle,
I'm tying on my roller skates.

My Grandmother crochets, finely, delicately,
coasters, doilies, tablecloths, bedspreads.

Her eyes scorn my Mother —
a piece of nothing she thinks.
Ethel Rooney, some Shanty Irish name she says.
She leans back on her platform rocker.
Nothing is bringing her a letter.
Rusty words roll along her tongue —
Is it from Babe? —
The words skip and tumble fractiously against
pressed unyielding lips,
words to be swallowed, not asked,
as her hand, dry as oak leaves in fall,
takes it from Nothing.

This is my house now, she sighs.
My son, my letter, my granddaughter.

This is my house my Mother thinks.
Billy's mother is welcome.
My Mother, once a Salvationist, is kind.

My Grandmother crochets.
There are no songs sung for her.
No one now to flatter her.
No Prince of Wales to dance
again and again with her —
the youngest M.P.'s wife —
no jealous eyes to covet her velvet and pearls.

My Grandmother Statira, is Kit,
second youngest of Joseph Shepard,

this December baby whose mother spent
one whole day, every other day,
riding south into York to the jail,
bringing beans and boiled meat,
waiting ... waiting ... for one half year,
Asking *Is Joseph for the gibbet like Lount?*

My Grandmother, enclosed
by the hot western sun, by her broken hip,
picks up the Shepard Prisoner Box,
holds it tightly, its message
fiesty and brave as her father:
Grant me indulgent Heaven that I may live
To see the miscreants see the pain they give.

Statira Catherine Gordon Cane, 1902. Grandmother of Vancy Kasper.

Grandma and Me

The house on Winona
stretched with silence.
Grandma not speaking.
Auntie, her sister, not speaking for seven years.
Vancy. Tell Statira not to leave the light on.
Vancy. Tell Auntie to close the door when using the facilities.
Crammed like needles on a hemlock branch
we set out two extra places every lunch
for the never-meet-your eyes
dirty-thirties drifters, knocking...

                softly knocking...

                    always knocking...

We mash a carrot with the oatmeal, subdivide
potatoes, water macaroni to feed them
in the kitchen, while Father, your son,
fully-suited in the dining room,
eats delicate bits of meat with the fat on...

                out of work for three years.

Later, neighbour women,
light-footed on the stairs,
mount to the back bedroom,
the one overlooking the football field.
Mother takes bets, one-eighth of a large penny,

odds on Oakwood kicking off against Central Tech.
She pours watery tea and reads the leaves...
                              Ireland sings through her skin
                                    cries out from her bones.

Today I forgive how you scorned her, instead
I look in this cemetery for the family plot where
the tall catalpa springs from your thighs,
wind riffing the leaves, giant hearts,
still green this fall.
I sit on the Shepard gravestone,
so far south from our land — from the street
named after us — deliberately misspelled—
from the mill and thousand acres that yoked
and sweated you — until you ran for marriage
into silks, amber and ivory,
living through and losing
two husbands, two fortunes
and I remember finally...
                        each night you lay me to sleep
                                    on a bed of poems.

Sunday in the Wartime Nursery

Aunt's fingers,
nicotined and yellow
match the chalk lines
on the fabric.
A smooth dart is not in the pinning.
A flat dart is not in the sewing.
She pulls and stretches,
lays the material under the needle. /
It's in the pressing. All in the pressing.
Her feet rock the treadle
back and forth   back and forth.
Then she holds up the pressmitt and spits on the iron.

Her niece, climbs up off the floor,
heaving and rumpled with cheap green garbardine
She is here for a reason
she only partially understands.

On weekdays, three floors below,
her aunt's hands, stiff and blue-veined,
beat egg whites with a fork.
Floating Island pudding for 67 children
whose fathers could be driving jeeps,
or mothers, lured by ambulances,
at the Bellevue Avenue Wartime Day Nursery.

Had her wrists forgotten those seven years
at the Berlin Conservatory?
She barely remembers her salad days;
her mildewed flat on Lindenstrasse
or Hans, whom she had kissed,
married and then left.

She's abandoned Greta, Reiner and Carl
whom she'd hugged, studied with, watched perform.
Her fingers still argue with Wagner
but she's misplaced any memory
of the Carnegie Hall debut, the ovations, reviews.

Her son volunteers for the RCAF.
Now at 18 he flies a Lockheed bomber,
low over Berlin blackouts.

She waits — lights another cigarette —
every Sunday, teaches her niece to be a tailor.
An international profession.

Claire Gordon McMaster. Aunt of Vancy Kasper.

John Montgomery, owner of Montgomery's Tavern,
great uncle of Vancy Kasper's grandmother, Statira Shepard Gordon Cane.

Nancy Wilket Shepard

She knew what she was getting,
marrying Thomas. Father-in-law Joseph, his voice
raised for reform long before 1803, the year of her birth;
their courting candle set by —
even their bundling bed —
manoeuvred around meetings,
secret forays, to change laws.

No, not like Great Uncle John Montgomery's wife
— how could she know her Reform man
would fight fiercely with his father —
hacksaw their Bird in the Hand Inn,
right in half — down to Newtonbrook ground,
go south, build Montgomery's?

Thomas, her heart of winter, her longest
night, had won her spiny nettle hand,
ruled by Mars, always
ram-butting against
rude roads and grudging teachers.

Nancy, his Aries thistle,
does not faint when Thomas is jailed
with brothers Mike, Jacob, Joseph
and Great Uncle John; instead

she gathers biting mustard, pungent
garlic, that Rebel women
will plant, come spring.

The dank and shivering Rebels —
mouldy, sang and sang,
carved their Prisoner Boxes,
tiny parquet messages of
love, anger, prayer,
lids sliding back and forth in compromise.
Nancy, over her morning-sickness,
stands in the April rain,
catches a box
under the south-west corner cell,
blue with hope,
cosseted by like Rebel women.

It was the scranch and rasp
of leg-irons clanking against Yonge Street,
down those three long blocks to the wharf.
Rebels with skeleton bones peered
from jackets hanging loose as
aged eyelids — and the dirty whisper —
Thomas to be shipped to Van Diemens…
Mike and John Anderson too.
Rebel mothers, wives, children,
dry-eyed with courage,
push soldiers back.
Van Diemens … wild with devils,
Kinkajoos, continent profound.

This new babbie, punches the
dough of her belly and jumps
to the Gaelic reel Nancy dances
to Her Majesty's stinginess —
too costly to ship 14 Rebels
to Van Diemens this year —

Thomas now crushed
with the others in one Fort Henry cell.
Seven-year-old Catherine and
James, five, know babbie
will be an Aquarius,
father, strange and stained.

Nancy trebles her work,
scours earth and water closets,
sprinkles lavender essence.
She boils rain-water to wash for five now,
— no britches to pre-soak —
looks for rubicund grubs under dust balls.
Her fat has fled these two years;
her flaying tongue
her loaded musket stops
Tory raiders at the bottom gate.
When she puts on her nightgown,
her bedroom is black with longing:
she, single; bed, double;
We live here she keeps saying.

The baby he has never seen,
his mother and Nancy
cross to Lewistown,
surrounded by Americans,
already arming, who cheer,
get ready again to invade Canada.
Nancy hears how Rebels
dug a hole, tunnelled out at night,
saved by pouring rain,
how Americans boarded them free.
She bruises his neck
with hoarded kisses,
wraps his brittle arms,
and hers, hard inside
their endurance, their heat.

These nights, so wild with
shattered celibacy, fingers,
lips, creating future destinations,
are enough. Nancy knows
Thomas must travel west,
chop cordwood for three years.

Finally she hears those old
Tories, General Thorne, Joel Harrison
have taken around their petition.
The Shepard boys finally
pardoned. Thomas home.
She: Double, bed: Double.

Tipperary Mary Switzer,
Streetsville, 1838

She's invisible, wife of
Martin (a Rebellion footnote — last man arrested)

I

It was Mary's own fault —
full of lust when she married the brawn of Martin Switzer.
But it was enough to make her
follow him right into his gift of gab and
up the gangplank onto that brig. 'Atlantic.'
She fell into his own storytelling:
"Sure and it's only a hop, skip and jump,
from Dublin here, over the sea to Boston."

Mary lost twelve pounds
somewhere in the fierce Atlantic.
Her stomach raked the back of her throat —
raw with the heaving of scraps.
Their baby gurgled and Martin rolled —
winking at waves higher than
any Celtic belltower.

II

Now in Upper Canada
Mary is that blacksmith's wife —
the pair of them Reformers —
but Mary wild enough to put William Lyon Mackenzie
in their spare truckle-bed for all seven days
of election week in Streetsville, 1834.
Martin's muscles had pushed Mackenzie forward
buck up against those Town Line Blazers,
every Tory packing tight his musket
and each barrel aimed at the Switzers.

Hadn't *she* left her windows wide those seven days?
Didn't *her* bacon and eggs waft their Reformer tang
across wheatfields and pigs into the nostrils of those
whiskey-drinking, fist-fighting Orange Tories:
Irish enemies of Reform.
Enemies of the Switzers.

Now there's a new Riding,
different boundaries.
Had Mackenzie won?

III

Like tinkers, the Switzer's had loaded and left pioneering —
sought the ocean air on Jersey's shore.
Damp, like Ireland, Mary said. *Like Tipperary.*
Mary's eyes lit like candles when
Martin set up as blacksmith.
She cocooned herself in her Tipperary lilt,
widened its vowels 'gainst that English/U.S. war.
But gossip burbled after their footsteps,
worms thrown up during 1812 storms.
"*We're Irish*," Mary repeated for seven years. "*Irish.*"

Memory of arriving in Upper Canada —
the name … Streetsville … birthed music to her tongue —
its paths, her lungs, throat, full
of the green smell of weeping willows.
Skirt whooshing, legs flying, she and Martin
jigged through mayapples and violets,
embraced the Irish lilt
of neighbours, their new country.
"*It's thanks be to Mr. High and Mighty British Consul in New York.*
Himself who granted this land to all us Protestant Irish."
Mary bent to their land,
and grabbed earth rich as blood,
let it dribble through her fingers.
She buried and stomped on her grandmother's goodbye:
"*Keeep your steel — a sharp knife you'll need*
fresh under your apron."

IV

On the wagon ride to Northern Massachusetts,
after landing in the New World,
the women's hands were raw as coral,
lye eating them as it did the shirts,
the breeks and nightgowns.
Mary saw her first jack pines, useless giants,
too woody for the fire and
too soft for building.
Blue jays (as young as she had been
leaving Dublin for Boston)
in their branches, cackling.

"'*Tis New Ireland,*" Martin said.
"'*Tis freedom.*"

What it really had been
was mud and drink,
being harnessed to the yoke
to help oxen strain and pull.
It was the loss of one babe in the womb
and watching another babe's breathing,
its lungs growing pus like dandelions.

"'*Tis shoreless land,*" he said.
"*New England town Meetings.*
Open for all to speak."

V

The violence … the hatred
on this Streetsville election night, 1834…
caused Mary's body to pucker,
her flesh, dry like neglected parchment.
Fear tripped and wracked
her wagon ride home.
So what if she had no vote…
her home … they knew where…
just down the road…
buckling under Henry Cole…
his Townline thugs.

But Mackenzie had won.
Reform skirts. Reform stays. Reform smiles.

Mary's hands stroke fine linen —
twelve yards for her daughter's wedding.
She and Martin sold two barrels of ashes
for six pounds, two shillings and three pence.
Martin buys a shilling of snuff.

VI

Two Tory ladies at tea:
"A ruffian represents us in the Assembly, Mrs. Rooney.
Yes. And I'll have another cup of tea.
A bad election. And didn't our band play so fine —
Protestant Boys and Boyne Waters.
Can you imagine that Mary Switzer
grinning while her giant of a husband pushed
that wild-haired Mackenzie right up to the polls?

Now, I know Mrs. Rooney, your man
was with mine the night our eight Blazers tore down
and broke up them fine iron gates of Switzers.
Threw them all over the road they did.
And did you hear one of them smashed all the windows in his smithy?
And hasn't he gone and offered a $50 reward?
He's a fool Rebel in this Tory Orangeman's land,
to think anyone would claim it.

Oh and I heard Mary Switzer
was terrified that night.
She won't be sallyin' forth
for too much bombazine for her hats
these days I tell you."

VII

Rebellion Thursday, December 1837:
    Mary's heart is fouled with worry.
        Its beat, yet strong, ricochets against aging ribs.
            Panting, Mary stows food, thrusts Martin out.
                Her silhouette stands tall in their dooway —
                    his footsteps westward towards Sparta,
                      towards Quakers there —
                        crunch, slide on the ice.

Hands cold, feet cold, Mary locks the shutters.
    At dawn she packs her muslin,aprons and one good dress.
    She whips the horses, runs the wagon
        to her married daughter's home.
            "Switzer forged pikes, ran bullets."
                Vigilante yells keep rhythm to axes,
                    help them hack Mary's lost door,
                      pry off half her roof.

Mary's terror drives Martin off, twice.
    She lies, tells each neighbour of her daughter's
        "He's gone over the border, into the United States."

VII

Rebel leaders Lount and Matthews hanged.

April, 1838:
Mary knew those three months
Martin was always on the run —
he sneaks back to tell her he's bought rough land —
forty miles west of Chicago.
She looks down at her hands, veined,
knuckles slightly swollen, knows
they will be raw once again, wonders
if they can yet do land scrabbling work.
In August, she welcomes Martin home
just before shots are fired into their house,
just before their son comes from Illinois,
is jailed at the border — *"I came to help them move."*
Just before Martin Switzer is the last man to be arrested —
just before Magistrate James Magrath acknowledges:
"Notorious Rebel Switzer might suffer local violence,
but there should be no lynch law here."

IX

What is the alphabet of hatred?
Deliberately enshrined by Tory violence,
it slows Mary's footsteps into church
that Sunday after Martin was jailed for treason.
Mary bows her head into the whispers,
into bold stares, hands up to mouths.
She prays. Sees Martin banging his hammer.
He stands in his own sweat, at his anvil,
voice booming, hands forging his own chains.
Martin in her eyes.
In her throat.

Joseph Shepard (1815-1899), great-grandfather of Vancy Kasper,
a scout for rebel forces on the eve of the Rebellion.

Labelled Rebels Forever

Like dangerous whispers
on an early December Tuesday,
800 Reformers and more,
gather down at Montgomery's
remembering cousins, friends
in England, who'd won their own march
— illegal and armed too — against
the Great Reform Bill.
Rising lions within their pride,
riding, marching, driven by
their children — until frothing
with muskets and grapeshot,
pitchforks and pikes —
draped in this devil's dark night,
they move through mud and snow,
as *coureurs du bois*, move;
— spread out as oxygen longing
to be breathed, spreads.

One steps, one shuffles, one stumbles,
uneasy why the Rebellion date
was moved up from Thursday.
Mile after mile, they barely pause,
stop for an ale at Montgomery's,
hear Anderson was shot by Loyalists,

hear Ryan, a Reformer, shot Colonel Moodie —
push off again south;
where Sheriff Jarvis waits at McGill Street,
already falling back after first volley,
running back into Toronto where
there were too few Tories that night
where Rebels could have taken Toronto that night.

Reformer's ragged front line, fire, drop flat
so those behind could shoot.
Mackenzie shouts, cajoles but his men
turn back, screaming
We've killed our own men,
shot our own Rebels.

Half-trained and badly led,
they curse the dark and lack of muskets.
Blacksmith after farmer after miller turn back,
and tramp mile after exhausted mile, back
north again to Montgomery's
where brave — but no soldier, he —
Mackenzie, a warrant on his head
for High Treason, waits for
his veteran Colonel Van Egmond.

Mackenzie drinks with his forces,
900 strong and rising,
Reformers, now labelled Rebels forever,
postpones the Rebellion for yet
another freezing day.

Maria Van Egmond, January 1838

(Widow of Mackenzie's ignominous chosen Commander)

She was curious about his close cap,
worn even under his hat.
On their wedding night she
tickled her finger along his body's
fourteen battle scars — too shy to ask
if his ears had been cut off,
this Maria Susanna Elizabeth Deitz.

       Today she does not cry.
       Her blood is German and she stands erect,
       coldly watches as Edward, their son —
       ordered by Dunlop (a joke), into the Tory militia —
       ransacks their own **Ross Inn,**
       confiscates his rebel father's papers.
       She turns away.
       Tomorrow they sieze our land.
       Thirteen thousand acres.
       No compensation.

God breathes hope into us, liebchen.
He smiles while I cut the **first sheaf of wheat**
in our new Huron county, *me with*
my plump strawberry cheeks,

still blushing, fat hands full of
virgin crop; you, my Colonel Van Egmond,
my forgotten man, so tall you bend down
from God to kiss my neck,
sweat breaking the rivulets of mud,
your tongue crusty with winter bread.

> *I, Maria Susanna Elizabeth Deitz,*
> *was wary of soldierly men but you were*
> *Count Anthonius Jacobus Wilhelmus*
> *Gisbert Lamoral Van Egmond,*
> *official at our German court of Mainz.*
> *Your Dutch lips, feathers brushing* **my** *hand,*
> *would slam commands and soldiers*
> *against Napoleon at Waterloo.*
> *Even your large nose held a certain electricity*
> *and you smelled of linden, not dirt.*

She barely remembers the Trail of the Black Walnut
her wet skirts, the other mildewed
Pennsylvania Dutch, trekking north.
> Waterloo County was lush, but
> John Galt's silken tale of the Canada Company
> led them further, to the Huron Tract,
> its million acres opening up.
> > Her colonel now Honorary Agent,
> > hires pick and shovel, constructs
> > the Huron Road, Wilmot to Goderich.
> > > She renders suet, draws whiskey at their tavern —

one of four inns her husband had built—
gathers wheat to feed her soul.

Mein Got! I was ignorant —
listening, lending — my door always open.
So many Company lies, promises broken —
Neighbors would be blind not to join us Reformers!
   They had elected my Colonel President
   of our Huron Union Society to
   protect us against injustice!
    *How could anyone **not** vote for mein Oberst*
    in this Huron District election?
     Dunlop! A low rank captain elected!
     Nothing has this Tory done!
      It is 1836 my colonel but you and I,
      we live in dark ages.
       We are Europeans. They whisper
       we never honoured the Crown.
       We are buried under Scots and Irish.
        Outsiders.

Now a Rebel woman, she knows
mischief and trouble strew Mackenzie's path.
But his plans make the trees hold their breath.
It's early December —
her Colonel, now nearly 70 —
rides back-shattering miles to Toronto;
sets the date for attack;
returns through that night to his Huron home.

She cooks sausage, sweet rolls, sugared coffee.
cushions his head as it falls on the table.
He snores and her hands fumble as
she wraps him in her knitted blanket.
He leaves again in five hours
plods back to Montgomery's Inn, for December 7th.
Her pillow is wet with sweat and nightmares.
She stumbles, spills whiskey serving at their Inn,
knows her Colonel will fall asleep on his horse.
She prays he will not
lose the road, drop .

This shrivelled corpse,
this bony sunken chest,
never lay against her breasts.
        Dazed, she wraps it in a fresh shroud,
          looks for ungent, pennies for the eyes.
            One leg, broken by the jostling of the cart--
              stuck out, trapped branches,
                caused her children to blaspheme.
                  Their icy January ride down to
                    Toronto jail, then home to Huron
                      was blustery and endless.
                  Never would **her** colonel veto
                  Mackenzie's plan to attack on December 7th.
          "Only 200 of us had proper arms," her son tells her, later.
          "Mackenzie raged, threatened to shoot him."

These tales are switches, whips to break her
   Someone is spreading rumors,
      She washes these fleshless limbs,
         feels sick, wishes Mackenzie had shot him.
           Jailed Rebels had shared their own bread
             but he lay with consumption, no rags to rest on,
           through the long January nights.
         She is alone now.
              Huron County Rebel wives and mothers
              hear the Militia reports;
                repeat behind cupped hands that
                  her Colonel swears *"I was kidnapped.*
                  "Rebels forced me to lead the fighting."
              Neighbors are laughing and only
           the memory of Catherine Shepard,
    risking her own life to hide him,
  comforts her.
                These disjointed bones,
                fought to defend Holland,
                survived Waterloo,
                were honoured by Britain and
                led our Rebellion.

Never was my forgotten man, my Colonel, tried for Treason.

Statira Catherine Gordon Cane (grandmother of Vancy Kasper)
with her first cousin, Letitia Bell (on the left) c.1880.

What the Women Knew About
Tory Champions of Law, Order

They were Reformers, suspects.
It was like living on the prairies,
nothing for women, children,
and their men, to hide behind.
Nothing to melt into, those months
after December Thursday
when all hell broke loose.
The Shepard's house had been
torched, Catherine was running
room to room, her arm
— both hands on fire —
no water, only hand-spun
blankets for the flames.
It's true it was a wet winter
and Catherine, not like them,
supported the armed Rebellion,
hid Colonel Van Egmond.

She knew that her floor was swept,
the cuckling and scutching of
her flax long since done.
A fire built high to warm his arms,
home after the long journey.
Still her sweat dripped into
twitching eyes, ran down dry flesh.

She remembered last May,
his whiskey-loosed tongue,
as he shouted "Those tickets old man
Bond Head distributes
were for phony land. Us Reformers were
cheated at the polls.
— Cheated when Mackenzie lost."

Historians say a bloody reign of
Tory terror did not take place.

She knew land and forest,
frothed Militia, tracking
shadows, ancient Rebel threats.
How could she or her children know
the Militia heard — a hint, a joke,
cackling whisper, a tavern lie —
that her family were Rebels.

She bundled and knotted
sourdough loaf,
Saskatoon berries and
sage against fever
for him to flee, him who was
not even in Toronto
Rebellion Thursday.
The proof he wasn't a Rebel —
new-blanketed horses outside, bought
and walked north from the Yankees,

whinnying hello
this snowy February 1838.

The knock was not her cheery neighbour
over the concession road
come to borrow flour.
She tries to tell them before
the stock of a Militia musket
splits her thigh,its bone shreds
now in her blood, swim
towards her liver her womb.
— Her breath gone, she hardly —
"My husband, was in Virginia,
bought the dun and the grey
tethered outside, rode them up
after the New Year from Virginia
— not even in Canada for Christmas
for the Rebellion."

Her neighbour's husband,
standing in the dun's stirrups,
cosseted by Tory Militia,
grins — that south-west corner field
husband refused to sell —
now his.

885 Reformers and Rebels,
husbands, brothers, sons
dragged into the bulging Toronto jail for

Insurrection or Treason.
Their women do not dwell
in the present. They churn, wash,
pickle and wait.
They dream waves of wood violets,
trilliums thick enough to wash hands in,
with their men home, turning fresh earth,
grinding axes, mending watches;
root and wild rose
clambering, modest, free.

No Whiskey for Remembrance

1.

Listen you blue-eyed lawyer,
assembling and re-assembling what you think is me.
What do you know?
Guarded you are
and falsely friendly.
Do you feel my discomfort?
My 89-year-old Aunty Tare, bedridden
in the nursing home I found for her,
has hired her own money-hungry member of your profession.
Her senile accusations say I stole her money —
forced me to hire you.
The ledgers proved otherwise.

2.

You are measuring me as I stand looking out your window.
I'm nine and Aunty Tare worked double shift
connecting detonators in a Scarborough munitions factory,
until early one morning at 4 a.m., waiting at the bus stop,
the woman next to her lit a cigarette and
blew her own hand off and half her face,
because after stripping and showering,
some particles of incendiary powder

had clung under her fingernails,
lingered lovingly inside one nostril.

3.

I'm eleven now, getting off
the streetcar at College and Bellevue,
almost knocked down by Wagner, thundering
out of a piano, the pealing bounces off
the firehall, hits St. Stephen's in the Field, Anglican church,
pulling neighbours with chairs to porches and lawns —
silencing even the firemen who whistle at the girls.

4.

I knew then, she knew
her only son was dead at twenty.
Killed in the War.

5.

Oh listen you blue-eyed lawyer, have you got a drink?

6.

I'm touching again the cheap gabardine
we cut out for my jumper that afternoon,
on the third floor of the Wartime Day Nursery,
where Aunty Tare was now live-in cook,
just after she dumped everything belonging to her son

into the garbage —
never to mention his name again.

7.

At thirteen, I went for lunch at the Toronto Ladies Club,
where Aunty Tare was manager,
her room exploding with flowers, floor to ceiling,
from a new lover.
One breast is always bigger than the other
she said matter-of-factly
when I was really worried about this.
I didn't know until I turned eighteen that her nude body —
portrait by Dorothy Stevens, sculpture by Frances Loring,
is in the National Gallery for all to see.
Or that she had been Varley's mistress,
the one he was *really* going to marry.

8.

She and I, only survivors of our Rebel Loyalist line,
reminisced about my father,
who wrote a *Rhyming Guide to Contract Bridge*
published by Eaton's, and once
hid Dozy Claxton's furniture in our garage,
one jump ahead of the repossession people,
because Dozy had been the finest
Royal Flying Corps Ace in World War 1
— before he hit the bottle and
was always drunk by 10 a.m.

9.

Oh listen you blue-eyed lawyer.
next time I ask you for whiskey —
don't lie to me about an empty bottom drawer.

Claire Gordon McMaster (Aunty Tare), on left with friend.

Toronto Ladies Club
Job Interview 1948

(told by Mrs. Claire McMaster to her niece)

I

Mrs. McMaster, we are delighted to have you apply to be
Manager of the Toronto Ladies Club.

Dorothy Stevens, the artist who is on our Board, has
recommendedyou very highly. I suppose you've heard the Na-
tional Gallery has just picked up six more of her etchings. I
honestly cannot imagine why the heir to the Eno Fruit Salts
fortune would choose to spend her time during World War I
drawing women working in a factory. I mean England was just a
step away from all that rotten meat that they say Flavelle sent to
the front.

Tea, dear? Thank you so much for coming here to Rosedale to
my small abode. I do hope it wasn't too too difficult with the
mountains of snow on Highland Crescent — oh my — you
didn't go to Highland Avenue by mistake! It's such a nuisance
when one's neighbours flee to Palm Beach for half a year.
Although none of us have used a sidewalk for months.

The Toronto Ladies Club is an oasis in the culinary desert that comprises theToronto of our generation. Even the York Club's dining room crumples before ours. And the King Edward need not even be mentioned. Our cook, Mrs. Dundas,highly tempermental, who is the veteran of several disputes with previous managers over whipping cream — she uses it exclusively — is the highest paid member of staff. That would include the manager.

Our Club rents from the second floor to the fifth, above the Toronto Dominion Bank where we have three guest bedrooms with adjoining bathrooms as well as our large corner dining room, private party rooms and staff quarters.

No one buys her way into the Toronto Ladies Club. That would be most crass.

We do not consider application for membership from indigent ladies as a negative thing.

Good manners, family background, artistic abilities are what counts, at 2 Bloor West, although in the case of Charlotte Whitten — such an entertaining woman — we made anexception to the four generation rule.

II

Now, I know it's rude to ask questions, but I must.
Do you cook, Mrs. McMaster?

Answer: I wouldn't dream of cooking, Mrs. McNisbitt.
Reply: Excellent. If you knew how to cook, Mrs.
          McMaster, we wouldn't even consider hiring you.

**I suppose like most of our members, you knitted socks and
packed ditty bags during the war?**

Answer: I connected detonators in a Scarborough
          Munitions Factory. Prior to that I was Den Mother to
          60 farmerettes who picked strawberries on their knees
          and other fruit through the summer until the apples
          were finished. They lived in barracks near the armed
          forces base at St. Catherines. I was given an adjoining
          office and bed-sit.
Reply: Most commendable. You were a Gordon —
          daughter of Statira Shepard Gordon Cane? Your
          grandfather was a close friend of William Lyon
          Mackenzie and I remember my grandfather telling
          me about himself riding with the Tories to rout out
          Rebels and jail them. Wouldn't it be funny if your
          grandfather was one of them? It is so comforting
          that Toronto is of a size that families really do know
          all the important things about each other.

**Do you know how to manage a staff, Mrs. McMaster? We
have four maids who live in and a skivvy who helps the cook.**

Answer: Mother employed a houseman and cook who were
with her for 20 years in Nanaimo and Vancouver. Two
came in daily. I learned from Mother growing up. Of
course my tutor, a Girton Girl, lived in as well.

Reply: A Girton Girl! My word, that's Cambridge.
Imagine one travelling all the way from England to
Nanaimo.

Are you able to budget for luncheons and dinners?

Answer: I'm a concert pianist. I studied in Berlin, Germany
before the first war. I have never budgeted for parties,
but to play well, which I do — I debuted at Carnegie
Hall—one must have a knowledge of mathematics.

Reply: Oh dear. We don't have a piano at the Ladies Club.

What about flowers, Mrs. McMaster, can you arrange them?

Answer: Of course. Mother had her own conservatory and a
huge garden on the west coast.

Reply: You are perfect for this post, Mrs. MacMaster. Just
what we have been looking for. When can you start?

Answer: I'm without accommodation at the moment…

Reply: Under the eaves on our top floor there's a tiny room
with a small bathroom adjoining and dormer windows
overlooking Bloor. Of course it gets a wee bit hot up
there…

MotherSong

for Ethel

Snowbanks are high, creased,
dappled with shadows.
No one telephones me here in Haliburton.
I pet the cat I share with my neighbour,
read poems by Tess Gallagher.
Tomorrow I will break trail,
ski all the way across Loon Lake.

The silence here is like
our Toronto house, Mother,
just after you died —
just after I shook you hard,
forced your cold lips open,
filled your stiff body with my breath,
filled your bedroom with my tears,
leaping off my cheeks to
cling to bedclothes, the headboard —
missiles of hope —
against my keening.

But I'm not afraid to be alone, Mother.
Today I feel your smile

warming my shoulders,
here in the mountains.
I will call my son in Halifax tonight,
and tell him how in 1945 you and I
once went all the way to Buffalo by train
and stayed at the Young Women's Christian Association
so we would be safe,
staying in a foreign country.

David William Gordon (Vancy Gordon Kasper's father), Royal Flying Corps, wounded and shot down in WWI, recovering in Ireland.

FatherSong

I walk a dirt road,
bluejays, crazy with crisis, scream —
panic ... dip ... retreat.

It's fall and I think of you, Father,
in hospital, wormy with
lumps that grew like mushrooms,
angry, stinking of lost
bowels, and pride.
Feel here and here you said.

The far shore is close enough
to touch today, and
fields sprout wild purple asters,
and crabapples drop
as I pass.

The Stranger came last night Father said.
He knocked three times.
I knew then I would take you to your home,
in spite of your specialist yelling at me in the hall,
his rage encircling, to keep us prisoners.
We smiled. I knew we knew
you would board the train and
the train would leave the station.

Once you were an Island boy
digging clams below Nanaimo hills,
licking salt from your skin.

On June 26, 1907, you sailed
aboard the Empress of Japan,
a cabin boy, bound for Hong Kong,
where you learned to eat
snake and thighs and how
streets could be prisons.

Two weeks later, as death
nibbled your lungs, you whispered
Americans. Landed on the Moon. Today.
I flew. Two wings and a joystick.
Then you peed the sheets.

The wind moves through burdock and creeper.
As I walk the road, I tighten
my sweater around my neck, and remember
you were the one who always called me Vance.

And I got to kiss you goodbye.

MotherMemories

I'm hungry for memories of you, Mum.
Not the Pond's Cold Cream smell or
the basin, between jaw and neck,
where the doctor tore out your glands —
but what you thought about —
grating cheese and breading finnan haddie,
listening to *Road of Life* brought to you by
D-U-Z, Duz, the soap that does
everything in your wash and
Crisco's Young Doctor Malone.
And too often waiting at night —
6 o'clock, 7, then 8,
until Dad phones, words swelling
his tongue, vowels, consonants,
ripping, stumbling, 'Love yuh Ethel.
Sorry, sorry, fell off the wagon.
Met this chap, Royal Flying Corps,
not my squadron, though,
lucky devil, he got out in one piece.'

Then an hour later, another call,
another hour, another call, until you
shut out the lights, turn off my father,
don't answer, tonight, through the night or
in the snarling morning ,when

500 boxes of Noxzema Skin Cream are
unloaded on our front lawn, amid
neighbours calling, my father's shaky grin
simmering — and you — the Winner,
grabbing both my hands,
twirling me in yet a new
Irish jig.

MotherSearch

Over and over I read her letters to me,
sent to Guide camp at Hawkesbury,
while I was waitressing in Lake Louise, or
visiting Aunty Babe in Philadelphia.
Nothing but the daily news there:
who came to dinner,
the dog got sick all over Dad's tomatoes, and…
please, please take care of yourself.

> You might ask why don't I know her?
> You might say what did I do?
> You might question where I was going and
> how did she have time to hang on —
> nail herself into my heart?
> "Fey," Cousin Em says, through
> breath thick as sour mash.
> "Just fey."

When I was five
we went fishing. Mom,
who couldn't swim, rowing lightly,
breathing her way across
a mirror, our wake closing
behind us like any entry
into her, like Georgian Bay

boulders and scrub shrink from
the right questions, never
warning me what I would never know,
or that Death lusted and would wait...
but not too long.

        Mother trolls for a muskie, the lure
        winking, hooks buried in
        green and silver.
        We would cook it over Balsam boughs
        flipping it over and over,
        soft and smelling of
        the Bay and embers,
        as later, we ate.

Ethel Rooney Gordon, Vancy Kasper's mother,
with Vancy Gordon Kasper on her lap in Georgian Bay.

Those are my roots, this is my garden with its various branches.
—Nancy Wigston, author

To the house of a friend, the road is never long.

friends forever

for Ayanna

she stands in the vestibule
this PAL Lodge — her building
for writers, artists, performers —
is not shaking;
it's whispers are muted,
maybe ... maybe ... they exhale
she half waves, stands
facing me, staring out,
tough, rooted as oak

friends forever
she's never clung to
my leaving before
my car is idling
i don't want to drive off
it's rooted to her curb
as i sit and sit

this rogue disease we share
plays, it waits...
doesn't know who to combust
yet...

Big Black Sunshiny Day

for Ayanna Black

My friend is wearing her brand new cap
as she lifts her arm, now savaged of flesh.
We are toasting the biggest black day in history.
"Remember that time I offered you South African wine?" I say.
"And you said, 'I hope you choke on it.'"
Our laughter has patina
on Obama's election day.
She sips — and these things within her, sip too.
She leans forward — her stick-like fingers
reach for some of my roasted garlic.
"When we met you had short hair," I smile,
as she fails to pat shorn dreadlocks.
Her cap falls off, as bald-headed now,
she looks up at the waiter, and orders quiche.
She knows these things inside
will enjoy eggs and milk so alien
to her 90 pound once rigid vegetarian body.
"You don't have the look, yet," I say.
"You got rid of it."

"But I eat for two or three now" she says.
"Here's to Obama, and to me not getting the look."

Forcing the Rogue to Wait

for Ayanna Black and Eckerhard Dolinski

The dreadlocks are gone and
my friend looks more like she did
when we first met. I reach
for her spoon, feed her rice with cabbage —
a little dribbles down to her rug, while
her fingers snake quietly towards my bread,
along the glass table top.
She doesn't see her own piece,
can't pick up mine. *"Oh sorry, girlfriend. Sorry."*
"The group is meeting at my place. Maybe you'll come?
We can pick you up first." I say.
Her eyes and mine lock in truth,
she smiles, says *"OK … OK …."*
"Thank God you've given up the wig," I say.
"You look like a Vogue model now."
Her snow white hair, sprouting like a
military crew cut, frames her high cheekbones.
A tiny layer of flesh coats her bones now,
her shuffle dance, holding my hands,
gets her to the couch where she sits
listening to me read her her own poems.

"We told you in 2006 we couldn't cure you.
But for two years we have
no record of any treatment at the hospital.
What's that all about?" Dr. Singh asks on her home visit.
Silence about: Women taking power over their own bodies:
About women making their own decisions:
About holistic self chosen treatment:
About forcing the rogue to wait…

We telephoned at least twice every week.
Now, some days she doesn't know me.

Ayanna's Slow Dance

for*Artist Pat Jeffries, ever there*

It's been a slow dance toward's this death of hers;
confounding her doctor who muses —
'She should have been dead months ago —
maybe we should do a study.'

Ayanna's apartment
beside the St. Lawrence Market is a magnet
littered with laughter, gossip and
parties — late-night — one, an all-nighter.
She sits, lies down or sleeps among her friends,
dressed in pink satin pyjamas,
and looking as usual, like a Vogue model.
They come before work, after work;
carrying macaroons, orchids and aloe vera in January;
I bring a chocolate birthday cake in February;
for him who hasn't left, hasn't fled back to Berlin.
He changes her sheets, holds her upright under the shower,
cleans up her shit, cooks her food, insists she walk a little.
The Government gives him a wheelchair after he asks and asks.
He walks her over to the Distillery; through the art galleries;
takes her aboard the ferry for an Island barbeque with friends;
brings her often to our place for fish stew, cauliflower curries.

She's losing her tongue, but not her smile.
"You gotta keep trying," she says. *"You gotta keep trying."*

Now all speech is gone.
On the thoracic ward last July, I held her hand.
Oh, Vancy, if I can live for a year, I'll be happy.
Six weeks later, she took off for Spain,
then London to see the Tate, then to Berlin
to stay with him, who couldn't, wouldn't leave her.

"I miss our every other day phone calls," I say.
"Me too, me too," she says and holds my hand so tight.

Doctors don't understand the staying power of joy.

Bequests

What about us, left here squabbling over your bequests?
You took a whole day out of your living time
to stumble around your apartment
point out, get your lawyer to write down,
file, and notify your powers of attorney friends.
Your closest one, can't take your furniture —
no place to store it...
"What's happened to her jewellery?
There was one pair of earrings..."
This African statue, too smooth,
no detail in the carving, is up for grabs.
Your CD's, left to your mate, are sorted into a carton;
he can't afford to fly them back to Berlin when he goes.
Fingers lift videos and tapes off the top, pocket them;
your yucca, orchid and swamp lillies are
left without water as if they too should wither, burn
as you did in that gray floored, cement walled furnace room,
cunningly concealed behind soft lit shelves in carved cases —
(the small chapel had cushioned pews);
your Tibetan priest chanted prayers
to carry you to the DALAI LAMA.
I'm crying, dodging as movers carry out sideways,
the mattress you died on.
I hug the African mask you left me — it's heavy.

I'm so touched by how you tried to repay all of us.
An only child out of Jamaica, with a little German
and some of Solomon's blood thrown in,
you carried a lifetime of generosity,
even into death.
We are so angry and bereft.

Ghazal

child thrown in, sink/swim on its own

moonrings
confuse solid, solid flesh

friends board a bus
to remote cities, leave no address

she waits
left with three computers, one word processor

genetic engineers
tell her the cardinal has options, one wing, no wing, deep
voice

maniacal stranger
crushes one lone black shoe lying in the feeder lane

Mother/me
he/she has two eyes, two ears, two arms, two legs

there has been no
terminal breakdown   yet yet yet yet yet yet
                yet
                    yet
                        yet
                            yetttt

friendsong

for R. S.

at the door to my study, you stop —
see scrummy kleenex sprouting everywhere
poems scribbled on newspapers,
tossed first drafts — I can see
you don't want to walk on my work and
you know there's an oriental rug under there
struggling its arms out around the edges
its patterns going under for one last time

I walk right over everything
lay the formal tea tray, Minton cups
its outrageous birds scream in butterfly yellow
as shyly I pour, for your first visit

later you take my poems to the piano
fingers thin as hope, running my words along keys
playing them in G, D, and A, showing me
a third voice buried

you ask if you could write a play about me
I said no

three a.m. when the telephone rings

I knew it would be you, fighting boredom
on the Hospital night shift, to tell me
you'd just met a man who lived
underground like a mole.

some days I feel your arm
resting on my shoulder
lines from your plays whispering, all around me,
as I walk down the street
alone

A Writer's Groupie

I look for her
sitting at every library Reading
night after night.
She draws a sandwich from her purse,
delicately finishes
with a minute to spare.
Some nights her face...
lines carved deep,
screams *"I'm tired, you buggers,*
cleaning your toilets,
wiping up your garbage."
I remember her smile
shimmer of joy, like rare
bloom of Christmas cactus.
She'd tell me I worked hard,
like she did, hard on the words.

Once, streets thick with rain, so empty of buses,
I insisted on driving her home.
Her anger grew and grew
as we drove so deep into poverty.
Ever polite, she stepped from sidewalk
into her one room.

My terrible mistake —
her dignity in shreds.

When I left, semester over,
she gave me the bookmark,
cut from a West Indian scarf, hand frayed,
carefully pasted dead centre
onto the book marker:
For Vancy, *best wishes*, then the date,
from Velma.

What We Don't Say

for G. R.

Branches and willowy tree trunks,
strain, reaching their white arms, hands
into the brown mass of barren valley behind.
Snow has etched their bodies beautiful —
you appear, all in black
from bellaclava to boots.
I'd just thought of you
sitting on a low wall,
shining more than the sun
down in Miami, near Seaworld
where your partner works.
    You say, *"I had to come back — mouth so full*
    of ulcers, I couldn't talk."
    We look at each other, you half smiling.
    I wait, my eyes pretend, my mouth pretends,
    my heart is too real for that shit
    and I wait.
    "Everyone's using these poles now,"
    you say, barely able to lift one off the road.
"The ski-pole walk," I say, *"you started it.*
Is anything better than a doctor
showing us the best way to walk?

Happy New Year," I kiss you on your cheek.
And I wait.
                    "*I'm back in Sunnybrook hospital,*" you say.
                    "*They let me and my liver out for today.*"
"*How about some of my chicken soup?*"
                    "*It's okay, Vancy.*
                    They take good care of me in the hospital."
"*I'm going away January 23rd — three weeks,*" I say.
"*When I get back, I'll pick you up.*"
                    "*It's okay, Vancy,*" you shiver,
                    now a step away.
                    "*See you in the park, before you go.*"
"*When I get back, for sure,*" I say.
"*For sure.*"

At the back, Helen Forbes (1912-2001) with Vancy Kasper (17 or 18 years old)
sitting just below her left shoulder, Red Rock, Sturgeon Lake.

Nothing Will Ever Be The Same

for Helen Forbes, 1912-2001,
Secretary, University of Toronto Schools

The sky is falling.
I am making parsnip and
apple puree for Christmas dinner and
I am not prepared.

The telephone rings.
The news is bad.

Helen has had a massive stroke.

Our home is not likely to
be crushed, but
the sky is falling.
Our basement is solid but
the outside walls could buckle,
hurt someone.

The grass is green at Helen's house and
ours — and springy.
It's easy this December 13
to dig, turn over, excavate.
What about the underground rivers?

The flash floods?
Will your children welcome us?
Next month? Next year?

Helen lies exhausted in Ross Memorial,
garbling, sleeping,
wrapped in diapers.
O Lady Helen, Lady Helen.

I was young when my mother died.
You took me, anguished, by my hand,
drove me north to your cottage,
Sturgeon Lake in January, solid, tranquil.
We saw a barn outside of Sunderland,
the farmer had painted *I love you, Marjory*
in huge white letters on the roof.

The sky is falling.
There will be no time for the
make-ahead, freezer-perfect mashed potatoes,
but maybe...maybe
the road between our homes will
still be short.

I will never see you again, Helen.
You will be walking Buddy,
still arguing with Ann about Santmyer's
And the Ladies of the Club,
embracing your own mother.

But I am in pieces.

There's no one else who knows I stopped
an Air Canada plane so we could
go to Expo for one day.
You couldn't find parking —
panting, I argued our case alone at check-in.
We boarded way out on the runway,
a make-shift ladder, especially for us,
dropped into our laughter.

The sky is falling.
I can't telephone you anymore
can't send you my stollens at Christmas
can't spread your fresh marmalade on my toast.

Can't hug you.
Can't hug.
Can't…

WidowSong

sandlewood
                    elusive   ever present
                                          as she
moves

   heralding
                 her entrances   her drifting
                                room to room

   when she died
                 her spirit   cool ribbon
                              along moon
streets

   she left me
                 her sandlewood jewel box

I refused
               to wear its contents
                                on grounds of

   spontaneous

          combustion

Where Did She Go?

for Helen Forbes, Dietician, then Secretary,
University of Toronto Schools

The fall day glitters hot
off Sturgeon Lake but chills
even the tar leading to the Point.
This September scene's too perfect.
Sighs, lonely and hurt, fall against
phantom footsteps, soft, behind.
I stumble. I'm alone ... I know
I'm alone.

The picture ahead's not idyllic.
Grass overruns the flagstone path,
double garage doors are wood-blocked,
Helen's Lindsay Post, plastic wrapped....
abandoned against the wet.

Maybe I was late for Helen's move.
I must have mislaid her address...
My coat hung on and off in her kitchen for 45 years and
I'm sure this is her tawny two-story cottage:
The one buffed by the onshore wind;
built on land claimed by her mother and father,
when they horse-drove their sleigh across the ice.

But there's no pungent smell of Buddy's Beef,
clink of teacups, laughter, not even academic arguments.
What about her children, Ann, Stuart, Bill?
Her grandchildren?
Did I miss a decision? Did I break a connection?

But I know, I know Helen's is the one
with three four-leaf clovers, thriving next
to the woodshed, next to never-blooming
hostas, deep shadetrees.
I walk between cedar hedges, while
the wide front porch, macabre and empty
faces the lake.

Waves hiss against rocks and
someone is sighing.
The living-room window
is locked. I don't hear her rise,
open the door, smile.
Eyes shielded I peer in.
Where is Helen's winged armchair?
What's that alien blue one?
It's stuffing's protruding from one arm.
The sofa the dogs slept on, has been evicted.
Her hand-knitted throws, gracing its back, vanished.

Maybe I didn't listen.
Where are her books, primrose, ivy?
Where has she gone?
Has she been there before?
Has she settled?
Is it familiar?

Notes on the Text

Rebel Women: Pennies are put on the eyes of the dead to pay the Boatman to safely carry the soul across the River Styx to Paradise.

My Grandmother Crochets: Husk is what is left after corn is shucked. Hasp is a building term, a fastening contrivance for doors. Prisoner Boxes were made in prison by the Rebels. They are works of art and were exhibited at the Market Gallery in Toronto last year.

Sunday in the Wartime Day Nursery: Salad days refers to being young. Up until 1942 when conscription was brought in, everyone who served in WWII volunteered.

Nancy Wilket Shepard: Courting candle was a circular iron band into which the candle was inserted to rest on a wooden peg. The peg could be moved up or down depending on how long the young man was allowed to stay. Bundling bed was a bed with a wooden plank down the middle, so the couple could lie together but not embrace. Van Diemens was Tasmania.

Tipperary Mary Switzer, Streetsville, 1838: The Switzers lived in Churchville, now Streetsville. Truckle-bed is a low bed on wheels that may be wheeled under another. Breeks were mens trousers fastened below the knee (sometimes spelled breeches, but pronounced breeks.) The 1834 election was considered a bad election by the Switzer's Tory neighbors because Mackenzie won 334 votes to his opponents 178. Bombazine was used for stiffening. The Switzers were hated because Martin had spread a false rumor, five days after the Rebels had been defeated, that Mackenzie, with four thousand men had conquered Toronto. Many Reformers, then took up arms and were jailed by vigilantes. Martin was blamed because he believed what lawyer Charles Durand had told him.

What the Women Knew About Tory Champions of Law, Order: Cuckling and scutching are different ways of beating flax.

No Whiskey for Remembrance: Dorothy Stevens is an artist famous for her etchings. Her work is in the National Gallery in Ottawa. Florence Wyle and Frances Loring are famous Canadian sculptors. Fred Varley, a painter, was a member of the Group of Seven.

MotherSong: My Mother had never travelled anywhere and regarded the United States with deep suspicion.

MotherMemories: My father flew in WWI. He was shot down by the Germans and thrown back into "No Man's Land" because his arm was crushed. He was rescued by a British ambulance and taken out to a hospital in Ireland.

Acknowledgements

I wish to offer thanks to the following sources of information and assistance:

The writers and editors of the following books, papers and articles: *Pioneering in North York; 1837 Rebellion Remembered*, Sesquicentennial 1837 Conference of the Ontario Historical Society; Thomas Shepard's account of the Rebellion in Robertson's *Landmarks of Toronto*; the acknowledged gratitude by W. C. Dent to Joseph Shepard who was still alive, for supplying him with several of the details in his 1885 account of the Upper Canada Rebellion; *A Farmer's Alliance*, Ontario History Volume XCIX, No. 2; *Dictionary of Canadian Biography* article on Joseph Shepard; "Inside the Old City Jail," *Toronto Star*, December 2007; *Everyday Life in Colonial Canada; Mount Pleasant Cemetery*. I am also grateful to those members of my family who kept letters and photographs and told the stories.

Many thanks to Gay Allison for her sensitivity in editing this manuscript. Ayanna Black, generous and bold, and Frieda Forman, with her meticulous eye and inspiring support, believe in these poems. Their extra notes, phone calls and comments were so helpful. Moral support and feedback came especially from Lorraine Williams and from my two writing groups: Ayanna Black, Sylvia Warsh, Heather Kirk, Pat Boast, Barbara Kerslake, Nancy Wigston and Pricilla Galloway; Sonja Dunn,

Pat Hancock, Barbara Greenwood and Jean Booker.
For their longstanding support, a special thanks to Tony and
Liedewy Hawke, Giselle Igiers, Margie La Flair, Elizabeth Mason,
Arlene Chan, Dorothy Milne, Cindy and Stuart Forbes, Corinne
and Bob Falconer, Nancy Smith, Susan Somers, Abbey Smith
Seguinot, Kathi Willing, Dino and Irene Voyatsiz, Marion and
Norman Childerhose, Rev. Jennifer Palin, Greg Robinson, M.D.,
Shirley Crombie and Anjie Rigopoulou. A grateful thanks also
to Maureen Talley and the Computer gang at Taylor Place.

I would like to acknowledge profoundly the poets who allowed
me to audit their classes at a time when I was struggling: Phyllis
Webb, bp nichol, Michael Ondaatje.

Poet, novelist and journalist, Vancy Kasper was born and grew up in Toronto. She received her B.A. from the University of Toronto and joined the *Toronto Star* as reporter, feature writer and columnist. Her articles appeared in magazines from Japan to Germany. An early member of the Women's Writing Collective, she is the author of a poetry collection, *Mother I'm So Glad You Taught Me How to Dance* and award-winning Young Adult Fiction, *Always Ask for A Transfer*, *Street of Three Directions* and *Escape to Freedom*. Her poems have been published in *Fireweed*, *Canadian Woman Studies/les cahiers de la femme*, *Quarry*, *Poetry Toronto*, *Waves*, and *Landscape* and broadcast on Canadian televison and radio. She has been a feminist for over 30 years.